THE BEATLES
LET IT BE

ISBN 978-1-5400-5740-2

For all works contained herein:

Visit Hal Leonard Online at
www.halleonard.com

Contact us:
Hal Leonard
7777 West Bluemound Road
Milwaukee, WI 53213
Email: info@halleonard.com

In Europe, contact:
Hal Leonard Europe Limited
42 Wigmore Street
Marylebone, London, W1U 2RN
Email: info@halleonardeurope.com

In Australia, contact:
Hal Leonard Australia Pty. Ltd.
4 Lentara Court
Cheltenham, Victoria, 3192 Aust
Email: info@halleonard.com.au

TWO OF US

Words and Music by JOHN LENNON
and PAUL McCARTNEY

DIG A PONY

Words and Music by JOHN LENNON
and PAUL McCARTNEY

ACROSS THE UNIVERSE

Words and Music by JOHN LENNON
and PAUL McCARTNEY

Slowly and smoothly

Words are flow-ing out __ like end-less rain __ in-to a pa-per cup, __ they

slith-er while __ they pass, they slip a-way __ a-cross the u-ni-verse. __

Pools of sor-row, waves of joy are drift-ing through my o-pened mind, __ pos-

I ME MINE

Words and Music by
GEORGE HARRISON

All _____ through the day, _____ I me mine, _____
All _____ I can hear, _____ I me mine, _____

_____ I me mine, _____ I me mine. _____
_____ I me mine, _____ I me mine. _____

All _____ through the night, _____ I me mine, _____
E - ven those tears, _____ I me mine, _____

DIG IT

Words and Music by JOHN LENNON,
PAUL McCARTNEY, GEORGE HARRISON
and RICHARD STARKEY

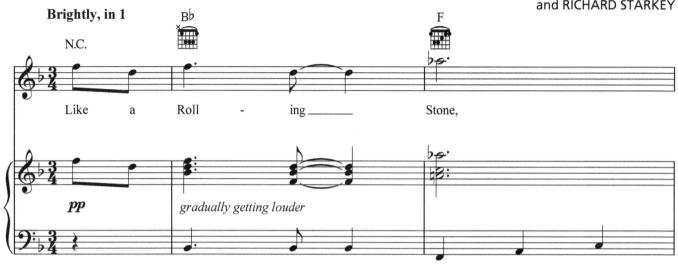

Brightly, in 1

Like a Roll - ing _____ Stone,

pp *gradually getting louder*

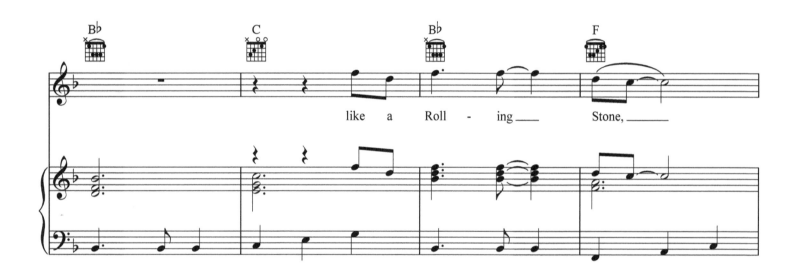

like a Roll - ing ___ Stone, _____

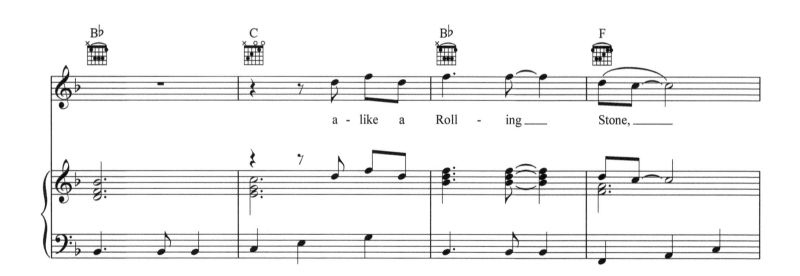

a - like a Roll - ing ___ Stone, _____

LET IT BE

Words and Music by JOHN LENNON
and PAUL McCARTNEY

When I find my-self__ in times of trou-ble,
Instrumental

Moth-er Mar-y comes to me speak-ing words of wis-dom; let it

be._____ And in my hour of dark-ness, she is

D.S. al Coda

CODA

Let it be, ____ let it be, ____ let it be, ____

____ let it be. ____ Whis-per words ___ of wis - dom; let it be. ___

MAGGIE MAE

Words and Music by JOHN LENNON,
PAUL McCARTNEY, GEORGE HARRISON
and RICHARD STARKEY

Moderately, in 2

Oh, dirt-y Mag-gie Mae ___ they have

tak-en her a-way ___ and she'll nev-er walk down Lime Street an-y-

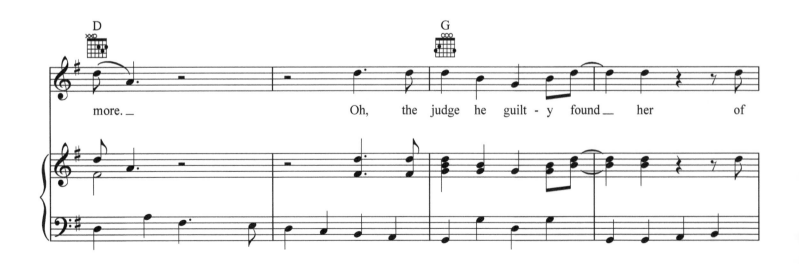

more. ___ Oh, the judge he guilt-y found ___ her of

I'VE GOT A FEELING

Words and Music by JOHN LENNON
and PAUL McCARTNEY

I've got a feel-in', a feel-in' deep in-side, __ oh, yeah. __ oh, yeah. __

Oh, please be-lieve __ me, I'd hate to miss __ the train, __ oh, yeah, __ oh, yeah. __

I've got a feel-in' that keeps me on __ my toes, __ oh, yeah, __ oh, yeah. __

I've got a feel-in', a

And if you leave __ me, I

I've got a feel-in' I think that

ONE AFTER 909

Words and Music by JOHN LENNON
and PAUL McCARTNEY

*Recorded a half step lower.

THE LONG AND WINDING ROAD

Words and Music by JOHN LENNON
and PAUL McCARTNEY

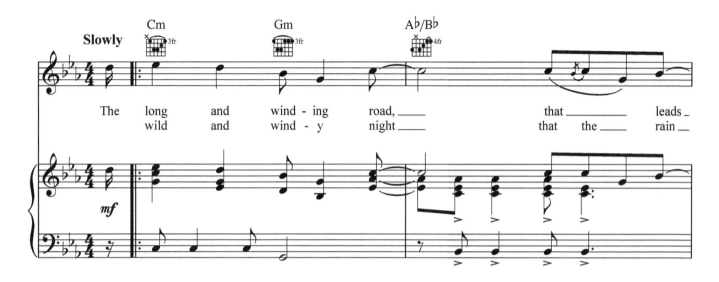

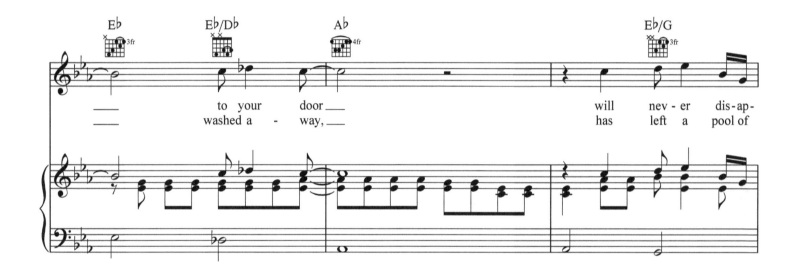

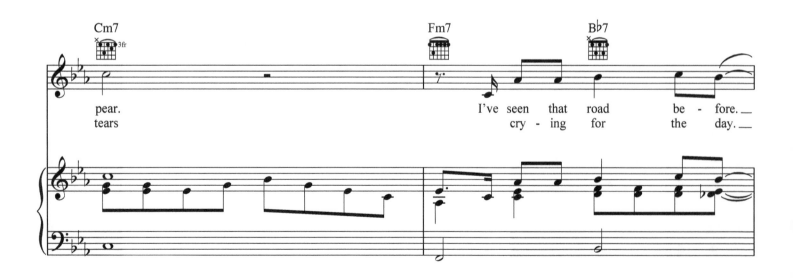

FOR YOU BLUE

Words and Music by
GEORGE HARRISON

(1.,4.) cause you're sweet and love - ly, girl, I love you.
(2.) want you in the morn - ing, girl, I love you.
(3.) loved you from the mo - ment I saw you.

Be - cause you're sweet_ and love - ly, girl, it's true._
I want you at_ the mo - ment I_ feel blue._
You looked at me,_ that's all_ you had_ to do._

_
_
_

I love you more_ than ev -
I'm liv - ing ev - 'ry mo -
I feel it now,_ I hope_

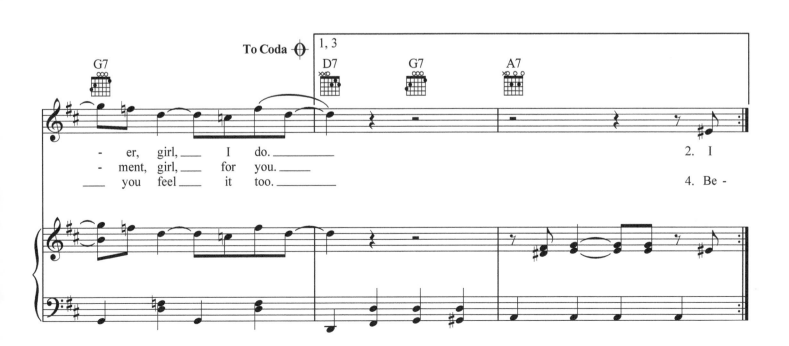

- er, girl,_ I do._
- ment, girl,_ for you._
_ you feel_ it too._

2. I
4. Be -

(Spoken:) Bop.

Bop, cat, bop.

Go, Johnny, go.

There go the twelve-bar blues. _

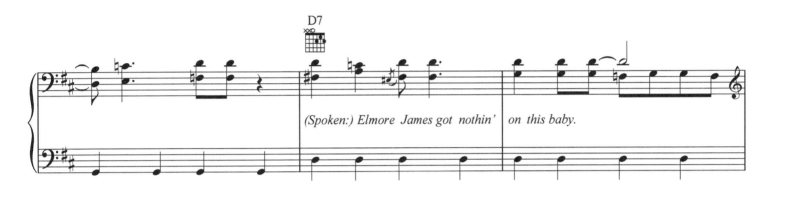

(Spoken:) Elmore James got nothin' on this baby.

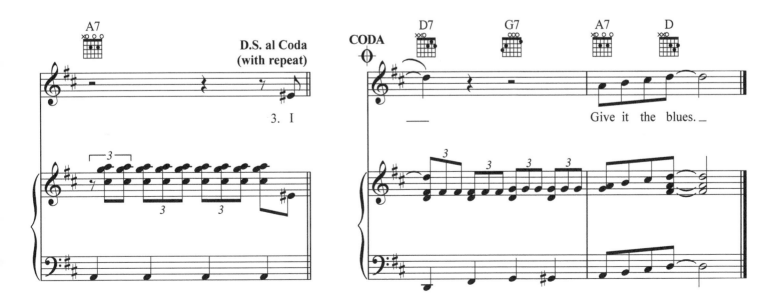

D.S. al Coda
(with repeat)

3. I

CODA

Give it the blues.

GET BACK

Words and Music by JOHN LENNON
and PAUL McCARTNEY

Jo Jo was a man who thought he was a lon-er, but
Instrumental
Sweet Lor-et-ta Mar-tin thought she was a wom-an, but
Instrumental

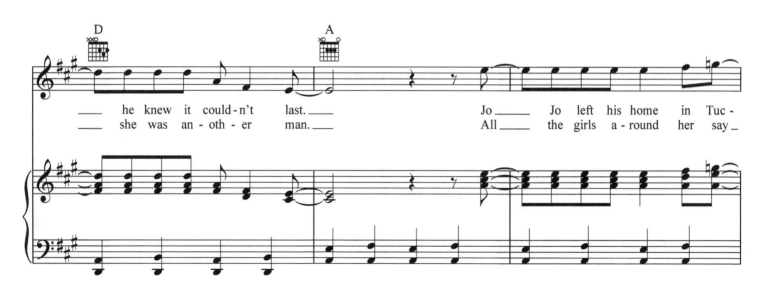

he knew it could-n't last.
she was an-oth-er man.
Jo Jo left his home in Tuc-
All the girls a-round her say

(Get back, Jo Jo.)

Spoken ad lib:

Get back, Loretta, your momma's waitin' for you,
Wearin' her high heel shoes and a low-neck sweater.
Get back home, Loretta.

Repeat and Fade